WPower

The Strength Of

An

EMPOWERED

Woman to Change the World

Companion Action Workbook

for

Personal or Group Study

____

First Name

____

Middle Name

____

Last Name

____

Nickname

____

Meaning Of Your Special Name

____

The Date You Start Reading

____

Date of Completion

Foreword

By Marilyn Bradford, Editor

The power of womanhood is evident in the author of *W***Power the Strength of an Empowered Woman to Change the World** and this accompanying **Companion Action Workbook**. The author, Felicha Sinegar-Stanley, is a woman of integrity, courage, strength, and most of all compassion for others. Her ability to empower women is built on a foundation of experience, education, and knowledge from years of research. She has an enormous passion to help women advance and thrive in life. This workbook contains many tools that has helped me to turn my dreams of empowering other women into action and results. Her greatest desire is that we will use these tools to become stronger leaders and then pass it on by teaching others their worth. Her vision goes beyond today but well into the future by promoting mentorship to young girls who will take the baton and continue the fight for women's rights and equal opportunities. Mrs. Stanley teaches us that this is not an endeavor for the faint of heart, but that we as women must courageously stand through our fears, insecurities, and challenges. I am encouraged by this study to do just that, realizing that "it is not about me" but that my plans must have a purpose of empowering others. She stresses the importance of not trying to go it alone. That we were built for each other and made better together. I just wish that I could be that fly on the wall of the many lives that will be changed by this study and go on to do great things. If only I could be there to witness YOU pivot from stagnant to motion, from contentment to change, from powerless to empowered and all those that you will take with you along the way.

Power – "to make the changes that transform our lives. I'm referring to the power to express more strength, confidence, authority, and impact so that we can overcome the obstacles in the way of success and fulfillment."

~ Kathy Caprino ~

This workbook was written with the intent to change lives by addressing your needs and empowering you with the tools and information you need to empower others to succeed. This workbook not only draws from the original book but incorporates fresh new information for a more comprehensive study. It is intentionally more interactive and engaging for enhanced learning, understanding and application.

We are very excited that this workbook is in your hands now. This means that you are ready to jump in and get started with great expectations and your head held high.

In WPower: The Strength of An Empowered Woman to Change the World Companion Action takes an in-depth look at the importance of women's empowerment and breaks it into manageable lessons for you. It will allow you to write down your thoughts and ideas throughout the book.

More importantly, it is designed to help you journal lessons that you can apply in your life today as well as other things that you can make decisions about in the future. This book will guide you on how to gain greater positive power and provide clarity about women's empowerment and the impact that you can personally make on another woman's life.

At some point, empowerment will come alive for you and there will be no stopping you because you will have your own mission for empowering other women.

*W*Power the Strength of an Empowered Woman to Change the World was written to shine a light on the many great contributions that women make in their everyday lives to reshape the futures of young women and children, strengthen families, build businesses, establish organizations, and fight for political gains for women. Many women affect change without even realizing their inborn power and abilities. WPower is a book focused on women empowering women and how vital it is on the world stage. Your endeavor to take this study to a deeper level by allowing this ***Companion Action Workbook*** to help guide you through each Section is a great step toward achieving the personal growth and empowerment that you seek.

What You Will Need

- ✓ Dedicated Time
- ✓ A copy of my book WPower the Strength of an Empowered Woman to Change the World
- ✓ Pen and paper for notetaking
- ✓ Or a journal for documenting this journey

Take Your Time - Read and reread again for a clearer understanding. Place a star next to anything that piques your interest in researching and learning more. Don't think you have to read it all in one setting because you don't. Take your time.

Highlight, Annotate and Take Notes - There will be specific points that may resonate with this particular season of your life that you will want to highlight and annotate. However, be prepared to take more detailed notes to help you to recall and apply what you've learned. According to Tim Ferris, in an article in Inc. Magazine, "taking notes is an essential step to getting more out of what you read".

Keep an open mind while reading - Don't read any portion of this workbook while tired, sleepy, not feeling well, or in a busy state of mind.

Take Action and Practice - Don't hesitate to remember what you've read, take action and put those great ideas into practice using them as often as you can.

Feel free to follow the contents consecutively from the introduction to the acknowledgments, or skip around, if you would prefer. The choice is up to you. When reading this book for the first time, I suggest that you read it in its entirety to take full advantage of this valuable investment of your time.

Table of Contents

Part One:
The Beginning of Empowerment

Read the section *Education and Empowerment* and answer the following questions.

1. Education is ____.

2. What are the two main traits that women need to succeed?

    __________________________   __________________________

3. What are some amazing things an educated woman will do for her children and family?

    ____

4. What is the most effective way to reduce poverty?

    ____

5. What are the two major elements in education and their impacts on women?

    __________________________   __________________________

    ____

6. Effectively educating ____________ ____________ and ____________ continues to be a challenge today.

7. Because education is very important in empowerment, we should start with __________ __________ and ____________ them from their teenage years.

8. Ways that women can empower____________ ____________ is by ____________

9. What it takes to be ____________ ____________ at an early age, as well as create a space where __________ can meet and __________ what is means to ____________ ____________ ____________.

10. Women leaders are now _____________ _____________ by reaching out to _________ on their jobs, in _______________ and _____________ places.

11. Empowerment is ____

____

Now that you have the gist of Women's Empowerment, what it is, what it's not, and how to share it.

Action Items:

 ➢ Do a Google search on women empowerment write down three different definitions, read them, and develop your own definition and write it below.

____
____
____

 ➢ Do a Google search of Women Empowerment businesses and write down the name and where they are located. Find one in your state and get involved.

____

____

____

 ➢ Reach out and find 2 women on your job or in your community who are empowering women. Write their names here.

_____________________________   _____________________________

 ➢ Look at your local middle & high schools in your area and find out if they are teaching young girls about empowerment of any kind. If they are, see if you can volunteer. If not, you may want to help start a program.

Feelings are about emotions, the innermost part of us that makes us human. How do you feel when you help someone?

____

____

How would you feel attending a conference where women are all challenging & empowering you to take that next step to start a business or attend college for the first time, or even still change careers?

____

____

____

When a woman is empowered by ___________ a _____________, watching a ______ or participating in an ___________, she gets __________ __________, __________ she needs to take __________ she __________ and take action to do whatever it is she wants to do.

When I woke up and realized that I could empower myself and it would help me empower other women, I did what?

____

____

____

____

LIST the 6 holistic approaches to empowerment!

1. _______________________________
2. _______________________________
3. _______________________________
4. _______________________________
5. _______________________________
6. _______________________________

Ask yourself this question and answer it here. Am I taking responsibility for my health and participating in political affairs or doing research on how to help my credit?

____

____

Think for a moment, would you like to influence the direction of social change that affect women?

____

____

What would you do? (explain)

____

____

____

S.M.A.R.T. GOALS

SMART goals are a tool that is used to plan and achieve goals. The S.M.A.R.T. acronym stands for **Specific, Measurable, Achievable, Relevant, and Time-based.** Goals can be used in every part of life. Most people set goals for business purposes, but they should also be set for personal goals. If you were to Google SMART Goals, you will find many definitions, but the idea is the same.

 Goals that are SPECIFIC have a higher chance of coming to fruition. To create a specific goal, one must answer these questions.

1. Who? What? Where? When? Why?
2. Who is involved?
3. What do I want to accomplish?
4. Where is this goal to be achieved?
5. When do I want to achieve this goal?
6. Why do I want to achieve this goal?

 Goals must be MEASURABLE having criteria for measuring progress. Ask yourself these questions:

1. How much /how many?
2. How do I know if I've reached my goal?
3. What is my indicator of progress?

 Goals must be ACHIEVABLE.

1. Do I have the resources and capabilities to achieve the goal? If not, what am I missing?
2. Have others done it successfully before?

 Goals must be REALISTIC, and achievable by having the necessary resources and time.

1. Is the goal realistic and within reach?
2. Is the goal reachable, with time and resources?
3. Are you able to commit to achieving the goal?

 Goals must be TIME-bound in that it has a start and finish date.

1. Does my goal have a deadline?
2. When do you want to achieve this goal?

On the next page is a goal sheet for you to use.

GOAL SHEET

List the personal (empowerment) goals you intend to achieve in the coming months.

1.

2.

3.

4.

List the goals you plan to achieve in the next year. Include the date completed.

Goal	Date Completed
1.	
2.	
3.	

List the goals you want to achieve in two years.

1.

2.

3.

4.

List the goals you will achieve in five years.

1.

2.

3.

4.

Plan B- How will you hold yourself accountable? What will you do if you fall short?

____

____

____

Takeaway

Now that you have been shown how education and empowerment go hand in hand, you know that women make up over 50% of the entire world's population which makes us leaders in education. Because education is very important in empowerment, we should start with young girls and develop them from their teenage years.

Action Items

- ➤ Find a teenage girl in middle school and talk to her about education and create a space where she feels that it's safe to talk to you.
- ➤ Find another teenage girl and foster an environment where she understands how to support another teenage girl.
- ➤ Use one of the above-mentioned teenage girls. Talk to the girl about finances, employment, and health.
- ➤ Take a young girl who's a relative or a daughter of a friend to a local college or university and have her talk to admission or advisors on the campus.

There are different definitions of mentorship but the one I like to use most often is Merriam-Webster's. The reason I like to use this one is because it's close to what I believe. The influence, guidance, or direction given by a mentor.

Write your own definition of mentorship HERE!

____
____
____
____
____
____

Mentoring is ____________, and it benefits ____________ and ____________.

You can be a _______ for ____________ inspiring others to use their businesses as a ____________ to empower.

Also, you can ________________ the next ________________ of women entrepreneurs.

Self-Check

If your best friend asked you to mentor her, what would you say and why?

____

____

____

____

Mentorship is an essential ingredient to success, and its importance remains the same regardless of the industry or field you work in. Mentorship gives women the tools to accomplish their ambitions while connecting them with other women.

Do you feel or know that mentorship is an essential ingredient to the success of women and if yes, explain your reasoning.

____

____

____

____

When women are connected to mentors they gain guidance, encouragement, and worthwhile connections that will grow and help them advance in their careers quicker than if they had not been connected to a mentor.

Do you think guidance, encouragement, and worthwhile connections are great things that a mentor should give to their mentees, and if so, why?

____

____

____

____

In my research, I have found that mentorship is so important that it can be a matter of success or failure in life or your career. In my first book, I talk about two of the young ladies I mentored for a few short years and how mentoring made a big impact on their lives.

From reading the first book, what are your thoughts about the things I did for both young ladies as their mentor?

____

____

____

Imagine had they never been exposed to a mentor what their lives would have been like today. We really don't know; we only know that they were empowered, and they have the tools to be successful.

What do you think their lives would be like today?

____

____

____

____

While we are on the topic of Mentorship, let's talk about Mentorship in leaders, students, and women in general.

The Purpose of Mentoring

To help the mentee tap into the knowledge of those with experience and expertise and learn from them to grow and become leaders themselves.

When I look at ___________________it started in my own______________ with me ______________________________my girls.

Research shows that mentoring in the past has its various forms and has been a crucial factor in fostering professional advancement.

Benefits of Mentoring

Here are a few examples: Being encouraged, empowered, achieving career goals, relationships, and leaning in.

Where Can I Find a Mentor?

- ✓ ______________________
- ✓ ______________________
- ✓ ______________________
- ✓ ______________________
- ✓ ______________________

10 Reasons Why You Should Become a Mentor

1. ____
2. ____
3. ____
4. ____
5. ____
6. ____
7. ____
8. ____
9. ____
10. _______________________________________

10 Reasons Why You Need a Mentor

1. ____
2. ____
3. ____
4. ____
5. ____
6. ____
7. ____
8. ____
9. ____
10. ____

5 Qualities That Make a Great Mentor (article)
Today's Christian Woman, July 28, 2015, by Diane Paddison.

1. Engagement
2. Objectivity and perspective
3. Thoughtfulness and introspection
4. Resonance
5. Honesty and insight

In addition, Paddison mentions how mentors can speak wisdom into your life, and they can be powerful catalysts for personal and professional growth. But not all mentors and mentoring pairs are created equal.

At one time when I was a mentee, I had a formal mentoring relationship. A formal mentoring relationship is where two people are paired either through their employer, church, professional association, or some type of group.

An article on the *5 Qualities That Make a Great Mentor* can be found at: http://www.todayschristianwoman.com/articles/2015/july/5-qualities-that-make-great-mentor.html

From my experience, I consider the following to be qualities of a good mentor:

- ✓ Willingness to share skills and knowledge.
- ✓ Shows a positive attitude towards the mentee.
- ✓ Have a vested interest in mentoring relationships.

- ✓ Demonstrate enthusiasm about her job.
- ✓ Values continued education in her field.
- ✓ Gives lots of guidance and constructive feedback on a regular basis.
- ✓ Respected by others.
- ✓ Sets and achieves goals.

Section Takeaways

Now that you know more about mentoring, especially what it is and the qualities of a great mentor, plus reasons why you should become a mentor, what actions will you take to move toward mentorship? Use the space below to answer.

____

____

____

____

____

____

Action Items:

- ✓ Do a Google search on the benefits of mentoring and write down the benefits you believe in.

  ____

  ____

  ____

- ✓ Write down what you have to offer as a mentor.

  ____

  ____

  ____

- ✓ Think about a woman who would benefit from your mentoring and take steps to connect and see if there is some interest in her being your mentee.

Here's a link to the National mentoring resource center.

https://www.nationalmentoringresourcecenter.org

What does empowering other women in the workplace look like?

(Circle all that apply) put a check mark beside the ones you plan to do.

1. Speaking up for her when she's not in the room.
2. Celebrate another Woman's strengths.
3. Connect her to the right people to help her.
4. Back her up in meetings
5. Support her when projects come up…Suggest her.
6. Be approachable and offer help.
7. Time spent working should be valued on quality over quality.
8. Be transparent about vulnerabilities and failures.
9. Talk openly about work salary.
10. Set up measurable targets so achievements are tangible.
11. Accept and embrace individuality.

In today's time, post Covid, there is a huge need even more than during Covid 2020…now that employees are being forced to return to the office, there will be fewer women returning. Who will empower women? It must be other women.

What is one of the things that hold women down sometimes?

____

What should women do to help other women in the workplace?

____

When you see or hear of another woman on the job going through difficulty, what should you do? _________________ _________________ _________________

What is another suggestion for empowering another woman? ___________ up for _________________ you work with

When women don't help one another and empower each other, everyone ___________.

Have you heard of Empowering Yourself? Yes or No (circle one)

If you have not heard of it, guess what? You may have to do it if no one is empowering you. That's a lesson I had to learn the hard way. Get up and do it yourself if there is no one around to do it for you. It's great to have someone empower you, but you are ultimately responsible for your own growth.

There are thousands of women's organizations and associations where women are looking for others to empower. Seek out what you need to empower ____________.

Do you really understand the magnitude of empowerment? Yes or No (circle one)

EMPOWERMENT CHALLENGE

(Details- You can set your own days or months for this challenge.)

1. Improve your health.
2. Get better sleep.
3. Commit to a new habit each day.
4. Read an inspirational book.
5. Create a vision board.
6. Commit to exercising 30 days in a row.
7. Take time for yourself.
8. Prepare & eat a balanced meal daily.
9. Listen to music.
10. Write down things you value.
11. Laugh about something funny.
12. Write down positive affirmations.
13. Stand up for yourself and others.
14. Surround yourself with supportive people.
15. Telling another woman a powerful story to inspire her.
16. Lift up another woman.
17. Give back to another woman in your own way.
18. Think positive empowering thoughts.
19. network with other exceptional women leaders.
20. Recognize Women of Influence.
21. Be empathetic and listen to her without judging.
22. Understand challenges and how they make her feel.
23. Keep your promise to her.
24. Be a mentor.

25. Encourage her by complimenting her on what she does well.
26. Be supportive without any expectations.
27. Encourage her to find her courage, confidence, and strength.
28. Empower her by sharing your knowledge.
29. Motivate her to empower herself.
30. Fight for her when she needs you.

Replace Negative Words with Empowering Words

As you say these words, pick out the ones that resonate with you the most, write them down, and use those for one month and then change and choose different ones for the next month. Continue this until you complete the year. There will be a chart at the end of the book for your convenience.

ACCEPTANCE, EXCEPTIONAL, INNOVATIVE, LOYAL, POWERFUL, GOAL-ORIENTED, GRATEFUL, EXCEPTIONAL, DESERVING, ACCOMPLISHED, AMBITIOUS, COMMITTED, LEADER, EAGER, COURAGEOUS, BEAUTIFUL, BLESSED, ADMIRED, ADAPTIVE, IMPORTANT, INFLUENTIAL, INTELLIGENT, AMAZING, BRILLIANT, BRAVE, CONFIDENT, FEARLESS, PHENOMENAL, SENSATIONAL, STRONG, TOUGH, AND WISE.

___________ ___________ ___________ ___________ ___________

___________ ___________ ___________ ___________ ___________

___________ ___________ ___________ ___________ ___________

Why use empowering words?

____
____
____
____
____
____
____
____

1. Write and speak these words to describe you and other dynamic women.

    ____

    ____

2. Write some Empowering words and affirmations. Start with the words I AM.

    ____

    ____

Songs That Empower Women

Empowerment Songs are good when you're not having such a good day. We as women go through many things and need a reminder that we can get through all things. Music is something that picks us up and changes our mood, makes us happy, and sometimes causes us to dance. Music is good for the soul and it's awesome.

Super Woman (Alicia Keys)	I'm Every Woman (Whitney Houston & Chaka Kahn)	Formation (Beyonce)	Run The World Girls (Beyonce)	Girls on Fire (Alicia Keys)	Shiny Stockings (Ella Fitzgerald)	I got A New Attitude (Patti LaBelle)
Feeling Good (Nina Simone)	Better Days (Le Andria Johnson)	Conqueror (Estelle)	One Wing (Jordan Spinks)	Overcomer (Mandesa)	A Beautiful Day (India Arie)	Optimistic (Sounds of Blackness)
I Am Woman (Emmy Meli)	I Will Survive (Gloria Gaynor)	Roar (Katy Perry)	"9 to 5" (Dolly Parton)	Stronger (What Doesn't Kill You) Kelly Clarkson	This One's For The Girls (Martina McBride)	Beautiful (Christina Aguilera)
I'm Coming Out (Diana Ross)	Good As Hell (Lizzo)	Survivor & Independent Woman Part 1 (Destiny's Child)	You Don't Own Me (Lesley Gore)	Respect (Aretha Franklin)	All About That Bass (Meghan Trainor	Born This Way (Lady Gaga)
I Am A Woman (Helen Reddy)	Hit Me With Your Best Shot (Pat Benatar)	I Like That (Janelle Monae)	U.N.I.T.Y (Queen Latifah)	Grown Woman (Beyonce)	Think (Aretha Franklin)	Proud Mary (Tina Turner

When a woman is _____________, she is ________and ___________to do what she needs to do. ______________a woman gives her the _______that she needs to get her _______started and _________.

Inspiration by my definition is to ________ ____________ into a person to get _______________out. Inspiration goes deep into your soul whether you know it or not. There is a deep connection between how a person's body and soul connect when inspiration happens.

Let me add a little humor to describe the inspiration for those of you who see humor in everything.

"The only place success comes before work is in the dictionary."
– Elbert Hubbard

"Too much of a good thing can be wonderful." – Mae West

"People often say that motivation doesn't last, Well, neither does bathing -that's why we recommend it daily."
– Zig Ziglar

Inspiration can be tricky sometimes depending on what you are inspired to do.

When you are asked if you can do a job, tell 'em, Certainly I can!' Then get busy and find out how to do it."
– Theodore Roosevelt

"There cannot be a crisis next week. My schedule is already full."
– Henry Kissinger

Support comes in many different shapes, forms, and sizes. I took the challenge and started a _________Circle. They are a small group of _________, ___________ who meet to _______ _______ _________.

______________are ___________ because they _____________ ____________ how to fight for __________ ___________ and other matters that ________ ____________.

Do this right Now! Google Lean In Circles! Answer the questions.

What is a Lean In Circle?

____
____
____
____
____

What are the benefits of Lean In Circles?

____
____
____
____
____
____
____
____
____

What do Lean In Circles Do?

____
____
____
____

____

____

____

____

____

____

What are some Lean In Resources?

____

____

____

Google LeanIn.org and read about the woman who started Lean In Circles (Sheryl Sandberg. Record the things that the two of you have in common.

____

____

____

____

____

____

There was a study conducted in 2022 about women in the workplace which tells us how far women have come, but we are still not equal, and many other great findings. I've provided a link to the eye-opening study by McKinsey & Company for your educational empowerment. http://leanin.org/wiw

"Women in the Workplace is the largest and most comprehensive study of the state of women in corporate America. LeanIn.Org and McKinsey & Company have published this report annually since 2015 to give companies the information they need to advance women and improve gender diversity. Over the past eight years, we have collected information from almost 600 organizations employing more than 20 million people."

Part Two:
Moving from Empowerment to Inspiration

When a woman is inspired, she is ________________ and ________________ to do what she needs to do.

________________ a woman gives her____ that she needs to get her project started and finished.

What should you say to inspire a woman?

____
____
____
____
____
____
____
____

What can you do to inspire a woman?

____
____
____
____
____
____
____

Who is an example of an inspiring woman you know or like?

____
____
____
____
____

What are three inspiring words and their meanings?

____

____

____

____

____

____

Name 10 inspiring women and their most inspiring quotes.

1.____

____

____

____

____

2.____

____

____

____

____

3.____

____

____

____

____

____

4.____

____

____

____

____

5.

6.

7.

8.

9.

10.

Name a woman who inspires you.	What does she do?	What is she good at?

What do you think she is inspirational?	Ways you can be inspirational.	What is inspirational to you?

Transformational: *(adjective)* able to produce a big change or improvement in a situation, a change or alteration. Some sort of change must happen for there to be a transformation.

Examples of transformation: Mentoring a young woman and she begins as a flower bud and after being mentored for a year she is now a full-blown Daisy. Another example is taking a shy freshman college student and mentoring her for six months. She is introduced to software developer classes and in the end, she develops an app that changes the world.

Now it's your turn to try and come up with some great examples of transformations.

____

____

____

____

In my book, I talk about an article I read about 6 Ways to Empower Your Employees with Transformational Leadership.

I thought I could

____

____

____

I will train them to

____

____

____

I began asking

____

____

____

I found

____

____

____

Transformational Leadership is an approach that causes change in individuals and social systems. It creates valuable and positive change in the followers with the end goal of developing followers into leaders.

According to www.Langston.edu, there are four factors to this transformational leadership:

1. ideal influence

2. inspirational motivation

3. intellectual stimulation

4. individual consideration

Do a Google search and define these four factors and write out an example for each.

____

____

____

____

In the book on pg. 41-43, I give examples of transformational leadership that I will use with my employees.

List some examples from the book that you may want to use with someone.

1. ___________________________________

2. ___________________________________

3. ___________________________________

4. ___________________________________

5. ___________________________________

Transformational

A BIG Change or improvement in a situation. How many big changes or improvements in your career or life can you name? For example, job promotion, purchasing a home, professional growth, positive thinking, and attaining a college degree. These are just some ideas to get you started thinking about some big changes that you have experienced. I want you to seriously take some time and think about your specific changes and improvements in situations that you had.

Write them here and say them aloud. When you hear yourself say them it resonates deeper in your spirit.

____

____

____

____

____

____

Don't underestimate how important transformation can be for your life. We need transformation in all areas of our lives.

Do you realize how transformational thinking can help you perform at your highest level and achieve great success?

The main word to keep in mind that must happen is CHANGE!

What are the 6 ways to Empower Your Employees with Transformational Leadership according to Drew Hendricks? Look it up on Google and list them here.

1.

2.

3.

4.

5.

6.

There are strong _____________ in all professions today. I challenge you to empower young girls and show them the way. What are some things that you can do to make this happen?

____

____

____

____

____

____

____

____

____

____

____

____

For starters, what is a shift? It's basically moving from one place to another, a change in direction or position.

Stories that are told can be very transformational and moving. Transformational ______________ can happen _____any ___and ___________.

It can _______up _______________which makes it ___________________.

What event did I attend that made a shift in my life? (Page 44)

____
____
____
____
____
____
____
____
____

Recall reading about a young girl named Paige on page 45 in the book. What was her shift?

____
____
____
____
____
____
____
____
____

What shifts do you need to make in your life right now? It could be a job change, relationship change, relocation to another city or state, change in lifestyle, or in your thinking. Whatever shift you need write it here and take steps to make it happen.

Let me talk about Shift in a different light. Adjustment in the way something is done. I believe that when we look at "Shift" in this way, we can also come up with many shifts or adjustments that we need in our life.

- Are you in a relationship that is not working or moving in a positive direction? A shift would make a difference for you.

- Are you in the same position at your job after 10 years? A shift would bring you a different outlook on your career.

- Are you communicating with people who are just taking advantage of you? A shift would make them see you for the great person that you are and not a pushover.

- Is your clothing wardrobe not attractive as it can be? Purchasing new clothing may be the shift you need.

- Is a friend or yours no longer being supportive and a good friend? You may need to find a friend who is supportive and values you for you.

- Is the neighborhood you are living in no longer safe? You may need to look for a better place to live.

- The ladies you go out to dinner with after work no longer seem to have good and wholesome talk. You may need to not go out with them any longer or find other ladies to go with.

- All shifts that you have should be positive and good for you, because if not, there is no reason to make the shift. I hope that you understand that I'm only giving you examples of the types of shifts you may want to consider.

After reading the shifts above, write out the ones that you need to do immediately.

____

____

____

____

____

Empowering women in your local community can be a process of providing support, resources, and opportunities for individuals and groups within a community to take control of their lives and achieve sustainable change.

- ➤ Validate women's self-expression
- ➤ Compliment her mind and soul
- ➤ Offer support to all women, even those who are strong
- ➤ Pass the mic
- ➤ Make sure other women have access to information
- ➤ Invest in women-run businesses
- ➤ Bring women into the conversation
- ➤ Directly thank women for their gestures
- ➤ Encourage each other to accept sincere compliments
- ➤ Call attention to other women's suffering
- ➤ Sponsor other women
- ➤ Go out of your way to make women feel good
- ➤ Volunteer
- ➤ Speak up about all issues
- ➤ Get to know your community
- ➤ Be a mentor
- ➤ Attend community meetings

The first major way in which I made a huge impact on women in my community is

____

____

____

Action Items

I need you to do some research on this one.

1. Go to your city's website and look for opportunities to volunteer to help women.
2. Call and make an appointment to meet with the person in charge.

3. From your visit decide how many hours or how many events you can do to empower women in your community.
4. Write your findings here.

____

____

____

____

____

____

Try this action item to empower women in your community:

Find a women's organization in the community of your choice. Contact the person in charge and let them know that you would like to give back to the community by empowering another woman through mentoring. Write the details here:

The name of the organization

____

The name of the person in charge

____

How many hours per week you will mentor?

____

What did you learn about empowering another woman?

____

It's your turn to decide on other ways to empower women in your community and list them here.

____

____

____

____

____

<h1 style="text-align:center">Lean In Circles</h1>

Lean In Circles is one of the ways in which I empowered women in my local community. Lean In Circles are groups of women who meet once a month to learn new skills and other professional development. Lean In Circles was started by ____ a ____________ of _________________ from ________________________ backgrounds, ______________, and __________ is what makes groups like this ____________ ____________.

Because I'm very passionate about empowering women in your community, I'm going to give you more ideas for you to follow up on or open your mind to other possibilities.

- ❖ Start a group through your local library
- ❖ Contact your local chamber of commerce
- ❖ Contact your local women's ministry at a church
- ❖ Contact women's service clubs
- ❖ Contact league of women voters

In the book on page 50, complete the following sentences.

One ______________, one of my ________________________ (__________) and I watched the movie ____________ __________________.

In the movie, ____________________ __________________ told a ________ lady she would not accept ___ ________ to be _____________without __________ all of the ____________ _________ ____________with her.

This is one ________ getting a ____________________and ____________ all other ____________with her.

Has there ever been a time in your life that you lifted or brought other women with you? If so, explain to her. If not, write what you would do and how you would do it.

____

____

____

____

____

____

____

____

____

____

____

Part Three: Maximizing the Empowerment

Do you know where the term 'Paying It Forward' came from? A lady named Lily Hardy Hammond coined the term way back in 1916. She used it in her book *Garden of Delight*. Since then, or shall I say most recently, others have taken the term and given it new meaning.

Paying it forward has huge benefits for everyone involved. In today's time, not only are celebrities paying it forward for others, everyday people like you and I are paying it forward in a big way. People with big hearts and making a difference for the next person in line. I'm sure you've seen great examples of this everywhere you go. During "COVID" pandemic times, I have seen and heard of people going to the extreme to make sure they help others whom they do not even know. I especially like hearing about paying it forward for women who want to go into business or who are educating women who are undereducated. I've paid it forward for young women who want to volunteer for a nonprofit organization and learn what it really means to impact the lives of others. I have paid it forward by mentoring women and empowering them to give them what they need to get started in their careers and in life balance.

Have you heard the phrase *Paying it Forward*? Paying it forward means helping someone else and that person in turn helps another.

Ways to pay it forward for women in need include:

1. ____

2.____

3.____

4.____

5.____

Have you ever paid it forward for another woman? If so, what did you do?

____

____

I can remember years ago when I needed assistance from _________ _________
_____________, they so graciously assisted me.

What are some ways in which you could help women in other countries?

1. ____

2. ____

3. ____

Ask yourself why it is important to help other women and write your answer here.

____

____

____

Name someone who has paid it forward for you to have access to education.

____

Who has helped you get a job?

____

Paying It Forward Quotes

"I've learned that you shouldn't go through life with a catcher's mitt on both hands. You need to be able to throw something back." Maya Angelou.

"When you learn, teach. When you get it, give." Unknown

"A woman with a voice is, by definition, a strong woman." Melinda Gates

"Motivation comes from working on things we care about, it also comes from working with people we care about." Sheryl Sandberg

LET'S GET EXCITED ABOUT IT!

This exercise will have you dig deep down in your heart for the answers.

1. How would you feel if you had someone on your job pay if forward for you to get a promotion? ____

Smile!!! Laugh!!!! Smile Again!!!

2. Think of a person in your church who needs you to pay if forward for her. Write her name here____

3. Think of someone you need to send a handwritten note to with great news introducing them to someone who has a car they want to donate.
Write that person's name here _______________________________________

4. Which organizations have been empowering women with the tools necessary to start a business? ____

5. On page 21, what are the words spoken _____________, _______________

_____________,_________________,_______________,_______________.

6. Anytime you take responsibility for your success, you can't

____.

7. How many women do you want to empower in your city? ______-_______

8. What is it that you need right now to empower you? _______________

____

____

9. Imagine yourself on stage receiving an award for empowering a woman who became a successful business owner turned millionaire. What would you do and say? ____

In this chapter, I listed several women who have empowered other women. I want you to write women you know who have empowered you and the area of your life.

Name of Woman who empowered you	What area of your life

In the book, Shelly Zali's article in Forbes on March 6, 2019, article entitled,

____

Shelly states in the article, ____

____

____

____

Should your voice be heard? _______________ Why?

____

____

Do you realize the "Power" that women voices have to make things happen? Have you noticed lately when women speak; everyone listens? Not just other women, but men and children too. Women, there is power in your voice!

There are many ways women let their voices be heard. List a few here. I will give you two to get your mind thinking.

Fighting for equal rights	Speaking up for diversity, equity, and inclusion

Name a few places where you can let your voices be heard and completion dates!

Tasks to Complete	Target Completion Date / Date Complete

There are a few things you need to remember when you are letting your voice be heard.

1. Make sure that your tone is right. It must be correct for the ______________ you're trying to convey.
2. When you are talking to someone, you must speak with _________________.
3. Always, Always, Always, be ______________________ before you speak.
4. You should always have an ____________ about every subject.
5. When you speak, make sure that you pay attention to your _______ language.

I will put a plug in here for Toastmasters International because they teach the above-mentioned. After doing it several times for practice, you like it and become good.

As women, we sometimes soften our tone when we speak. Don't do it!!! Just come out and say what you need to say. Instead of being afraid to speak boldly, allow your confidence to shine through showing the best sides of who you are.

What is your story? Everyone has a story to tell. Your story is just as important as anyone else's.

____
____
____
____
____
____
____
____
____
____
____
____
____
____

Have you ever used your voice for those who cannot speak? When I say those who cannot speak, what I really mean is those who are afraid to speak, feel that they are powerless, those that are in the minority category, the less fortunate, the uneducated, and finally; those who are immigrants to this country. Explain here.

____

____

____

____

____

____

____

____

____

Would you like to use your voice and speak for those who cannot speak for themselves? What are you going to do? Write it down. Make it a goal. You owe it to yourself and others.

____

____

____

____

____

____

____

____

____

What causes are important to you? For example, American Heart Association, Domestic Violence Prevention, Saving the Children, Fighting Against Cancer, and Arthritis Foundation. Whatever causes you support, I say let your voice be heard and be Active!

____

____

____

____

____

____

____

____

Here is a list of "Strategies to Make Your Voice Heard" (Forbes, July 10, 2020) written by the Young Entrepreneur Council. After reading each strategy you will have a chance to write what you will say about each one.

1. Introduce yourself and speak confidently, be concise, to the point, and direct.

    ____

    ____

    ____

    ____

    ____

2. Start with active listening. Listen to what others have said, then reflect on them. When you speak, be certain and don't hesitate.

    ____

    ____

    ____

    ____

    ____

3. Speak loud and clear. It gets people's attention.

____

____54

____

____

____

4. Use your voice to offer value.

____

____

____

____

____

____

5. Be prepared.

____

____

____

____

6. Ask questions.

____

____

____

____

7. Maintain confidence regardless of what someone else says.

8. Silence your inner critique putting your feelings of self-doubt aside.

9. Trust Your Ideas. Use creativity and innovation as a denominator of your thoughts.

10. Seize the opportunity.

____

____

____

____

____

____

____

11. Use the 'Yes, And' Approach

____

____

____

____

____

____

According to Sheryl Sandberg of Lean In, there are three ways she knows that men can empower women ____________________.

1. Vocally _______   _______   __________ for their ideas.

2. Include ___________   ____________ in conversations about

   ____________________.

3. Include ____________ in social ___________and ____________________.

It makes sense for men to empower women. List the women whom men can empower.

1. M_ther
2. S_ster
3. A_nt
4. G_rl-F_i_nd
5. Female C_u_i_
6. M_th_r-i_-L_w
7. S_s_e_-i_-L_w

Write out how you want men to empower you.

____

____

____

____

____

____

____

____

____

____

There have been men in my life that have empowered me. The first man in my life to empower me is my Lord and Savior Jesus Christ. The second man in my life who empowered me was my earthly father. After these great men, there are my uncles, brothers, and a host of friends.

Each man has empowered me in different ways, but I can honestly say that the empowerment given was positive and made a difference in my life. It can be healthy for a man to empower a woman with what she needs. I tip my hat off to husbands and other men who empower the women in their lives. That strong relationship that you have between the two of you makes it great.

At work, I had a great gentleman who empowered me by the name of Dr. _______ _________. I will never forget how he took me under his wing and gave me the support I needed as a colleague. I was very ____________to him for that. Even with any relationship, men should invite women into the conversation about opportunities.

If you have been empowered by a man, share your experience(s) here.

____
____
____
____
____
____
____
____
____
____
____
____
____
____
____
____
____
____

Part Four: Equality & Power

Let me first make the distinction between equity and equality. Equity means everyone is given what they need to succeed. Equality means being equal in status, rights, and opportunities. Each person is given the same thing regardless of anything else.

Define equality in your own words!

____
____
____
____

We as women want _________________in ______and _____________________
in the _________________. Women want to _____________________________
_________________ equal to a man _____________the _________________
job. This is only fair for women to want and get. Women have been fighting for this right for hundreds of years and we are still not there yet.

It is alarming to find out by research that __________ pay more for _______________________items than men. That's not fair and it's definitely not right.

Now is the time for ___________________ to get paid equal to a _____doing the same _______.

We should continue to _______until we have ___________everywhere that we _______.

It is so ___________________ until we have_______, _______, _________, as well as ______ our

Elected _________________to do _____________________.

List the names and titles of your local, state, and federal officials you can contact about equality.

____
____
____
____
____
____
____

Women have _________in __________side by side ___________men but still have _______received the __________ _____________________that a man has gotten.

Why do you think this is happening?

____
____
____
____
____
____
____

Do you think that one day men will wake up and say, we will allow women to compete on an even playing ground? Yes or no (circle one) then explain why or why not.

____
____
____
____
____
____
____

What are you willing to do to be a part of this change?

____

____

____

____

____

____

____

Most women want equality in the workplace. This is because for many years women have not experienced equality in the boardroom. Women should be paid equal to a man doing the same job. Have you heard of the Equality Act? Women we really need to know our human rights.

Do a Google search for Equality Act 2010 and write it here.

____

____

____

____

____

____

____

____

____

What are the protected characteristics of the Equality Act?

____

____

____

____

____

____

The Rule of Equality (https://en.m.wikipedia.org)

Equality before the ____________, also known as ____________________under the law, ________________in the __________ of the law ___________ equality, or legal egalitarianism, is the _____________ that all people must be equally ______________ by the _____________.

There are two main types of Equality.

Social – equal opportunities for all people, jobs, club memberships, and promotions

Political – access to the same processes and opportunities; the right to vote or run for a political office.

List 5 examples of equality

1.

2.

3.

4.

5.

Why do we need equality?

____
____
____
____
____

Equality Now is an organization that supports equality for women. Their tagline is very timely for today, it states, "A just world for women and girls." Their vision is a world in which women and men have equal rights under the law, and full enjoyment of their human rights. Their mission is just as focused as their vision. It is to achieve legal and systematic change that addresses violence and discrimination against women and girls around the world. How awesome is that? (equalitynow.org)

After visiting their website, I feel that you will be compelled to get active in the fight for equality because you will understand the reason for the urgency.

Women overseas make about _____ percent less than women in America according to a report from the United Nations International Labor Organization. Throughout the few pages on equality, you will find some alarming statistics, and this is just to open your eyes to reality.

When we as ______________ ________________ one another, ________________ happen.

We can't wait for _____ to wake up one day and say, ______ ______ allow women to ________________ on an even ________________ ________________.

What are you willing to do to be a part of this change?

____
____
____
____
____
____
____
____
____

Another place that women are in the minority, is the news media. Women of Color make up a small percentage of the news media according to Women's Media annual report. Think about all the women who attended college and planned to have a great career in this industry. What can be done to increase the number of minority women and women of color who get into this industry to at least 45% or 50%?

____
____
____
____
____
____
____

Not only is this the case in the news media, but it is also equally stunning in the number of women in the tech sector. Even after two years, women still fall behind men in this industry. According to techfunnel.com, the latest statistics are that women barely make up 25% of the workers in this industry. What's interesting is that women in their twenties are increasing the female presence in the tech world.

What do you think of when you hear the two words Salary Negotiation? I've talked to women about it and most of them do not feel that they can successfully negotiate the salary for a job position. The main reason given is that they don't know how, and don't have the confidence that they can do it and get what they ask for.

Salary Negotiation is important to women. Yes, some women are afraid and a little apprehensive when it comes down to negotiating. I too at one time didn't know how and felt that I lacked confidence. The changing point for me came from participating in webinars with successful women who explained how they got to the point where they could go into a negotiation and demand a greater salary than what was offered or even demand the salary that they knew they deserved. Imagine that you are the person going into a job interview or even going to your current boss and successfully negotiating the salary you deserve.

Wake-____ women who have not been on the front ________ ____ for ________________. Get ____and ______up for what you want. What I see is a few ____________standing ___ the ___for ____ of us.

What are you doing about equality? Are you sitting on the sidelines? When are you going to get up?

____
____
____
____
____
____
____
____
____

Women's Empowerment

My definition of women's empowerment is when you have the power or the authority to stand up and either voice your demands, argue for other people, and make a difference for the ______ of _____________.

We as women have the ____________ to act at will. What does that mean to you?

____

____

____

____

____

Our __________________________________ matters because that's ____________ beginning of our growth. There has been some improvement in the last 10 or 15 years but we should be farther is ______ ______ of full ___________________________.

"The U.S. Agency for International Development (USAID) affirms that gender equality and women's' and girls' empowerment are fundamental for the realization of human rights and key to effective and sustainable development outcomes."

This means that for societies to thrive, women and girls, men and boys, and gender diverse individuals must have the agency, social support, and structures to make their own choices and live free from violence and abuse. They must have equal rights and opportunities as well as equal and safe access to and control over resources. They said it best when they said, "Achieving gender equality in society will improve the overall quality of life for ALL people throughout their lives."

This is an actual policy that supports advancing gender equality and women's empowerment around the world, not just in other countries. This is the kind of information we don't hear about unless we do some research. I don't know about you, but when I was getting my master's degree at Texas Woman's University in Denton, TX it was a degree requirement that you took and successfully passed two research classes. Today, I am still thankful that these two classes were added to the degree plan.

According to Resonance Global, "There are four areas for women's empowerment, and they are climate change mitigation and adaption, digital development, global supply chains, and safety from gender-based violence." After reading deeper into each one of the four areas, the one that resonated first with me is digital development. This is because there are more men online than women and the reason why it's all about sociocultural norms, lower digital literacy, and lack of aces to critical enabling devices. I feel that I have a lower digital literacy than most men. I work with men all the time and they seem to know everything about the digital world.

According to Resonance Global, there are some strategies that can be used to advance women's empowerment in this area:

1. Improve women's access to information and opportunities via digital solutions. This mainly affects women in developing countries and rural communities everywhere. This limits women's ability to engage in income-generating opportunities such as working from home or having a side gig that can be done on the computer from home. Basic digital technologies provide an opposite direction, connecting women to market information, new economic opportunities, and nutrition and health services.

2. Digital financial services can unlock women's access to finance. Digital financial services include alternative credit scoring, and assets as collateral were previously a requirement.

3. The anonymization made possible through digital tools can help combat implicit bias. E-commerce and digital financial services have a unique and important role in minimizing implicit bias that stops women business owners and sales executives from getting financing or making sales.

4. Women and Supply Chains companies are now seeing how barriers put in front of women are stopping progress toward advancing sustainable and ethical supply chains, and they have begun setting new priorities and initiatives for women's empowerment.

The solutions to all this and how companies can invest in empowering women are to do the following:

1. Include women's voices to shape new solutions. This means putting a plan in place to ensure that women's voices are heard. Having our voices heard is important to us.

2. Equip women with the skills and conditions they need to survive. That is exactly what women's empowerment is all about. You must invest in women by training them and giving them the tools to succeed. I've said this repeatedly. In addition, invest in a safe and equitable working environment for women, to promote participation in the supply chain. Provide gender sensitivity training to stop stereotypes.

3. Partner to co-create better solutions and scale impact. There are a few companies that are already doing it successfully. The partnership should also be with the company's own suppliers. The ones that they are already doing business with.

4. Addressing Gender-Based Violence and Safety. What needs to happen here is empower women leaders and community champions who are in the trenches and leading organizations to drive the change.

5. Promote the best practices by implementing them through local changemakers.

It is in every person's best interest for women to be empowered and empower other women. Women's empowerment needs to start with young girls. When young girls get it and know what they can do from an early age, they can begin making a difference at a time when they are growing and nurturing their

_______________.

When you do a Google search on women's empowerment, you will find women's empowerment conferences, workshop ideas, women's empowerment speakers, various types of women empowerments, women's employee empowerment, empowering organizations, and the list just goes on and on. With all the above mentioned, it tells me that women's empowerment is huge, important, and growing every day.

There is so much to be said about women's empowerment, how it started, how it's grown, where we are today, and where we are headed. My main reason for imparting a lot of information here is that it's changing daily.

Conferences to Attend
For those who have a real passion for empowering women.

- ❖ CGCM Connect 2 Empowerment Conference. This is an empowerment conference designed to propel Professional Women Forward Naturally and Spiritually.

- ❖ Juraim Organization for Youth (JOYE) Women Empowering Women Conference. This conference's focus is on personal development.

- ❖ I'm My Sista's Keeper Conference.

- ❖ I CAN DO Women Empowering Conference. Women to walk in their purpose.

- ❖ Gender Equality and Women's Economic Empowerment Conference.

- ❖ Faith City Church Women's Empowerment Conference.

- ❖ Women In Business Empowerment Conference. Positive impact on your business.

- ❖ My Pain Has Purpose Women Empowerment Conference.

- ❖ Women Evolve Conference.

- ❖ A Woman's Worth. Rise, Thrive, & Elevate! Women's Empowerment Conference.

- ❖ Venice Area Women Empowering Women.

- ❖ Extraordinary women empowerment Conference. Anointed Praise & Worship Ministries.

- ❖ Metro Technology Women's Empowerment Symposium.

- ❖ Virtuous Woman Houston Elevate Higher Empowerment.

This is not an exhaustive list and I do not endorse any or all of them, I noticed when doing my research that this is a list of empowerment conferences that are available to attend.

This world is changing every __________________of the day and we must change the way we look at _______________. Because women have more options and opportunities, today is a better place.

Some women tend not to like change unless we are talking about clothing, shoes, houses, and possible situations. We need to look ___________and _______________it.

Digging deeper into world changes, reveals a stark reality. Women have been passed over and held hostage for hundreds of years. Now we can break free and run with urgency. Wake up, my sisters. Men have been empowering other men for decades.

It was S________________ of 2019, I finally decided to make a change and lead a circle group of women for Lean In. Lean In is Sheryl Sandberg's most successful work. This is the kind of empowerment that makes working with __________ all the better.

I had no idea that God would have me leading such a prestigious group for a highly respected lady. I mentioned before, Sheryl Sandberg is one of the women who I look up to as a role model as well as Melinda Gates and others. Being a role _______________ or __________ is very important to the success of empowering someone.

P_______ is a strong word with a strong meaning. ______________ to ______________ is quite different than power to a man.

Question *(Get ready for it...... Prepare your mind...... Here you go...)*

Why are women in power hugely important???

Studies and statistics show that women leaders help increase productivity, enhance collaboration, inspire organizational dedication, and improve fairness.

Do you agree with the studies and statistics? Explain

____
____
____
____
____
____
____
____
____
____

Have you heard that only 10% of Fortune 500 companies are led by women? Does that matter to you? Why?

____
____
____
____
____
____
____
____

Women use power in _______________ways to show their strength. I saw a
P___________ P_____________ presentation by Kathy Caprino, the career
C____________, and I was amazed at how she put power into perspective. Caprino
said, "Power is an essential component to a thrilling and impactful career, but
many women shun it.

I use my power to help others and not tear them down. It gives me the ability to
achieve, generate, and manifest strength to do good work, and inspire others to
make an impact for change. And, I gain the authority to lead and work as I please.

If you were to use your power to help others, what would you do?

____
____
____
____
____
____
____
____

Power is an amazing thing when used the right way. When I feel powerful, I feel
that I am doing something worth doing, I earn respect and I am recognized for a
job well done. When I share with another woman a word of encouragement and
give her a hand up and not a handout, I feel amazing.

What can you do to give another woman a hand up?

____
____
____
____
____
____
____

Women wake up and realize that we are greatly blessed with talents, skills, gifts, abilities, and the power to do anything you put your mind to. Now more than ever women are speaking up for themselves and the causes that matter most. When we talk whether it be to our boss at work, or people we meet on the street, or even a group of men; we should speak with power in our voices and be confident that whatever we say we will be heard and not just seen. Do you believe this? Why or why not?

____

____

____

____

____

____

____

We must be brave to speak up and be heard. These past few years there have been several women highly visible in the public who have spoken powerfully and who have made things happen for the best. Many women are afraid to speak out powerfully, but I am not one of them. I challenge you to speak up and be heard. I want you to speak to others in the workplace, in women groups, and to anyone who will listen. Make it happen and record your results here.

____

____

____

____

____

____

____

____

____

____

I read and learn from many people, some famous and some not so famous. You can tell people who speak powerfully by the message they deliver and the way it resonates with people. As I think about positive ways in which I have used power to make a difference in a woman's life, I think of a time when I talked to a young lady about a time when I had to be brave and speak up for women who have been in domestic violence situations.

Here is another challenge for you. Find a woman who has been in a domestic violent situation and speak a powerful message to her and encourage her to speak up for herself and other women in the same or similar situation. Record specific details of your communication here and share it with others.

____
____
____
____
____
____
____
____
____
____
____
____
____

There are many different sources of power. There is electricity, physical force or strength, reward, coercive, legitimate, referent, informational, and expert power. All leaders should have the last six types of power. To be a good leader one must know how to use power.

Power is necessary for enacting change in any situation. I could give you many examples of the power that I have used to be impactful. I have used the power within me to impart the power to others by speaking life into another woman's situation. The choice of words being used and the vivid images from the words spoken are more powerful than one can ever imagine.

I learned about the power of positive thinking and speaking through Norman Vincent Peale. He wrote almost one hundred books on positivity and how powerful it is. I use the power to create such a force within someone by giving them what they need to get started in reaching their goals. It's almost like a life-and-death situation. **Action is required here!!!!!** I Need YOU to list some positive words that you can say to other women that will change their lives. To do that, I need you to think positively first and then prepare what you will say. Write it out here.

____

____

____

____

____

____

____

____

____

____

____

____

My influence over the women whom I communicate with allows me to use my power to help them. Sometimes the help is in the form of connecting women with other women and other times it may be showing them a skill. I sometimes use informational power to give a woman information that she can take and learn to use for her purposes. Other times I have used reward power where I have rewarded women for completing a college degree or a particular course that will enable them to grow professionally. I tell you power is astonishing when used the right way to give another person a hand up and not a handout. Think of 5 things you can do to reward another woman. List them in order of importance here.

1.____

2.____

3.____

4.____

5.____

I went on Christmas vacation, and I came across a few women that I felt I needed to give the power to for them to be successful with their new year's goals. One especially stood out because although she lived in the mountains of North Carolina, she was very open to hearing my ideas and she immediately said, "How powerful." I said to her, Power is great if used to empower another woman.

As a leader, I choose to utilize legitimate, expert, and referent power. The reason I say that is, legitimate power is having a position of power in an organization. I have been in many women's organizations and held different positions. This can be helpful when you need to introduce women who need to be empowered to other women who can empower them. In my everyday walk, I use legitimate power and the results are good.

Let's have you consider ways that you can use legitimate power here.

____
____
____
____
____

Next, I use my expert power by sharing my experiences and knowledge to help women in all industries with empowerment. I have worked in many industries and consider myself an expert in education, food service, business, childcare, management, and speaking. Now only those areas are mentioned, but I also use referent power because I am trusted and respected by my peers.

Just as I have had you do before, come up with your own ways on how you will use referent power to help other women. Once you have decided how you're going to do it, write it down.

____
____
____
____

Now, I hope you get the idea of the types of power I used to help empower other women. Women do not take power lightly; often it takes strength to make it happen.

Part Five:
Leaning in All the Way

To me, Lean In means to get in the game and make it happen. Every woman has the power inside of her to do what she needs to do with a little help. As a career woman, I have experienced trying to climb the career ladder without help and I can tell you it doesn't always work. It would not be difficult if you have other women to help you and are happy to lift you up.

Who will you ask for help?

____

____

As far as women's rights and equality, all women should Lean In and put forth an effort to empower another woman. Whatever expertise you have, use it to pay it forward for another woman. Imagine the impact you can make on women globally by putting forth a little effort. It does not take much to make a big impact. My plan for women everywhere is to find out what I can do to make their lives better and just do it.

Because equality does not happen in silo, what group or organization will you join to fight for women's rights and equality?

____

____

____

Because there are no boundaries on where you can go globally, what country will you go to and connect with women to help them and make a difference?

____

____

____

Yes, women, we can lead by example, and we will have many generations of young girls turning into women coming behind us who want to impact others. I especially charge women between the ages of 30 and 50 to create your group of women to pour into. Sheryl Sandberg did and now she has hundreds of Lean In Groups all over the world and they are making a difference. I know because I am a product of one of her Lean In Groups in Dallas, TX.

Look for a Lean In group to join or start and talk about it here.

____
____
____
____

We must stir up the will to lead in women who may be apprehensive, afraid, or need a little push. Some women may have all the tools necessary to empower women, what I say to them is do it even if you are afraid. We are not bold in every situation that comes our way. I can't tell you how many times, I have been afraid to fail, and I started a business anyway. When I failed, I got back up and started over again. If women all waited until they no longer were afraid or received enough money to fund their business for 5 to 10 years, or until they received a business degree…. we would not have many women-owned businesses. With the power I have inside of me, I will never stop making a difference and being a positive impact in the lives of women.

Write a statement of confidence telling me what you're afraid of and how you are going to do it anyway. This is the only way. Once on paper, you will feel empowered to step out on faith.

____
____
____
____
____
____
____

There is a blessing in helping other women reach their goals and dreams. When someone sets goals that are important to them and doesn't know where to turn to for help in reaching those dreams, they die. Imagine the confidence level of that person. A woman needs to have a high confidence level to set herself up to do anything she puts her mind to. It takes confidence as high as the tallest trees in the United States.

Do you have the confidence that it takes to help others? If so, explain.

____
____
____
____
____

**If you feel that you do not have confidence at this time,
I will ask you to repeat after me.**

I know that I can help other women reach their goals and dreams because I have what it takes to be successful within me. I don't have all the confidence at this time, but I will be there soon. I want to be a blessing to other women, and I will start right now with what I have.

As a young girl, I had this idea that I wanted to be a big and important person. Some of my friends wanted to become teachers, or dancers, and me, I wanted to be a fashion designer. Well, my desire only lasted until my second year of college. After that goal did not last, I had another goal of being a physical therapist. My dream was not nurtured but smashed by a college faculty advisor. A college advisor is a person whom students meet with to get advice about their academic program. This person is required to give the student the best information available. An academic advisor is like a high school counselor that you would meet to discuss your dreams of going to college and getting a great job. You would spend a great amount of time with your college advisor.

This was an opportunity where I should have been empowered to reach my goal of becoming a physical therapist. This is one of the points that I'm trying to get across to you. People should look for opportunities to make a difference in the life of someone else. The things you do can make a difference in whether a person's dream comes true or is crushed. This was a lost opportunity and sometimes that person may never get that chance again.

What would you have done in this situation?

____
____
____
____
____

No woman in my family had ever talked about goals or dreams that I can remember. That's what I mean when I say if you have no one directly near you to tell you about goals it does not just come naturally to you. After living life for some years, I realized that other women came into my life and made it possible for me to begin thinking of new goals. When I began going places and traveling and meeting people who were educated or had an interest in lifting me, things changed.

Name the person or people in your life who poured into you.

____
____
____

There is so much beauty in helping others until I know that God ordained it. The amazing thing about helping others is it causes you to appreciate and be thankful for what you already have. What are some things you are thankful for?

____
____
____
____
____

It can also give you a sense of renewal to get back to feeling like yourself because life can make you feel down sometimes. I know it may sound crazy but, helping others can help you live longer. When you help others, your body releases the hormone that creates harmony. Just think about that for a moment. It's beautiful to live longer by giving a woman a hand up, not a handout. There is a big difference between the two.

When you volunteer in any capacity, regardless of where it is, and there are people all around you, altruism has a contagious ripple effect. I have volunteered for The Family Place, an organization that empowers victims of family violence by providing safe housing, counseling, and skills. This creates independence while building community engagement and advocating for social change to stop family violence. Just knowing that I was a part of the healing of women and children made me feel like I was impacting their lives in a way that mattered.

Others see the good that you are doing, and they want to join in. Most of the time when I did any volunteer work, I had my four little children with me. Yes, all four grew up and today they are volunteering at places they like and what matters to them. I would tell all my girlfriends that I was going to this food bank in Plano, TX and I looked again, I had everybody at the food bank, or the women's shelter, and everybody was having a good time. This work is inspiring and heart-touching to see in action, even just one time will do.

As I volunteered as a woman in many places for women, I have made friendships and they became strong friendships where both parties contributed to keeping a mutually beneficial relationship going. I began to feel like I could take on the world and that is such a great feeling.

In the process of empowering women, I feel a sense of belonging. Each time I support, volunteer, and share my gifts with another woman I feel that I am exactly where I should be. I get a sense of purpose and satisfaction from knowing that I have helped someone reach their dreams and goals and you can too. A dream is part of a person's life that cannot be separated. People's dreams are real, and some do come true. Have you ever heard of Joseph in the bible and how he dreamed that he would someday rule over his brothers, and they hated him when he shared his dream with them?

Dreams are significant and strong as Joseph's in the bible. Dreams give specific instructions and can warn of danger too. In this situation, Joseph was hated for his dream, but it didn't stop him from dreaming. This should be a lesson for all of us. Not everybody can accept your dream and it's not for everyone to understand. Don't let others stop you from dreaming. Joseph's dream came true. He dreamed that his mother, father, and brothers would bow down in front of him (Genesis 37: 1-11) BibleView.org. You must chase your dream no matter what it is.

Women should pay attention to the details of their dreams. Write down the details of your powerful dream in a journal book that you can refer to later. There are many lessons I have learned from my dreams, but the most important lesson is all dreams are from God. I am the only one who can tell others about my dreams. No one else can experience the beauty of my dreams, but me. The bigger the dream, the bigger the experience. Small dreams never got me anywhere.

I had to fight for my dreams to make them come true. Dreams are beautiful and lovely. Dreams opened up a new world for me. One of my biggest dreams is to be able to empower thousands of women all over the world. Another dream of mine is to win the noble prize for helping others. I've talked about dreams and the beauty of empowering women because it is just that.

In a way, beauty and empowerment are related because it's the quality present in a person that gives intense pleasure and satisfaction to the mind, body, and spirit by making a difference in the lives of another woman. This comes out when I go and help other women reach their financial fulfillment so that they can purchase a home or save enough money to put their child through four years of college.

Another example is how I feel when I help a woman who has been in the workforce for forty years and has never attended college before; earn a degree that will elevate her and give her options to either stay at her current job or look for a better one. I have assisted young women in college who were able to get scholarships and receive an internship at companies like Disney and Amazon. The amazing beauty is the satisfaction of knowing that I had a part in helping her get to that next level is a great feeling in my mind and spirit. My love for people, in general, is what I think about when I look for ways to go all out for women. We are special creatures and when we are provided with what we need to flourish I love seeing the beauty that comes from hard work. If you are a woman reading this book and understands how it feels to help your sister, aunt, goddaughter, granddaughter, or girlfriend, you know how it feels to be a part of the lives of millions of other women.

My eyes open wide when I think about empowering women whom I've never met or been in another country making a difference in the lives of women of many different cultures. I have always wanted to travel the world and meet women in other foreign countries and hear their stories. There is beauty in knowing that it's amazing when women come together to make a difference in many ways. I'm on a mission to meet and dramatically impact every woman with all the strength I possess. When I put my strength against any force that comes my way, I know I will be changing the world in a big way. I'm talking about mountain-moving changes. Close your eyes and imagine the beauty of the mountains in Washington State or Colorado, or even Iceland. I am not only interested in changing the world where women gain additional rights but also to empower women to help others with a domino effect.

Key Lessons for Empowering Women

✓   **Find out what she needs first**

✓   **Provide her with helpful resources**

✓   **Advocate for women's rights**

✓   **Have open communication**

✓   **Provide accountability**

✓   **Get women into decision-making positions**

✓   **Actively participate in social justice**

✓   **Instill confidence in her**

✓   **Teach resiliency**

✓   **Teach self-motivation and self-awareness**

✓   **Provide the skills and training needed**

✓   **Share degrees of power with those on a lower level**

✓   **Try new ideas**

✓   **Show her how to build a network**

✓   **Be her support person**

✓   **Provide her with the tools to be successful**

- Build your professional network of successful leaders.
- Get out of your own way and start thinking positive.
- Find a mentor who has been where you are trying to go.
- Be intentional on how you show up.
- Learn the behavior and qualities of good leaders and follow.
- Build a powerful support group of people you can call on.
- Volunteer for the position that leads to a leadership role.
- Join organizations and take on opportunities to gain experience.
- Attend Women Leadership Conferences.
- Look for a YWCA workshop in your area.

I believe in empowering women. Why? Because empowering women works.

When women and girls are supported or empowered, they gain the tools and resources to speak up for themselves and advocate for others who do not or cannot speak up for themselves.

Women's empowerment is important, and it matters to those who know it, believe in it, and need it in their own lives.

I believe in empowering women because an empowered woman can change things! This is a testimony from my own experiences. When women are empowered, everyone benefits – families are stronger which leads to stronger communities, and builds into stronger villages, cities, states, nations, and yes, the world!

I believe in the power that comes from empowering women to not only reach their goals but helping others reach their goals too.

Ultimately, empowered women take the time to experience happiness and to inspire others to find fulfillment in life in an ever-changing world. Changing the world can happen one person at a time or with many people at a time. You determine how you will make a difference and just do it.

Part Six:
Women's Economic Empowerment

➤ Establish goals/plan (personal and professional)

➤ Seek out a financial planner/analyst (find someone you can trust)

➤ Save first, spend later (you should always save for future)

➤ Own your financial situation (know where your money is coming from and where it's going)

➤ Make the financial market your friend (have a diversified portfolio)

➤ Speak Up (talk about money)

➤ Go for balance (a balanced lifestyle is a wise lifestyle)

How the Nonprofit Came from the Book

I believe that I should first tell you a story of how the nonprofit idea came from the book. One day I was thinking that the book is just a stepping-stone for a chance to reach and impact as many women and girls as possible. I looked around and then inside and said to myself, a really good way to take it to the next level is to start a nonprofit for women and offer the services you know women need. With my educational background, I knew that education is the key to going places or making things happen. Wanting to advance women and girls and assist them in reaching their goals, I knew this was a great way to do it. I called a few women I knew and told them about my idea and the plan I was thinking of, and they gave me support and thought that it was a great idea. I called my mother and shared the idea with her, and she was very supportive of the idea. Shortly afterward, we decided that Women Empowering Women would be a great name for the nonprofit. I reached out to SCORE to get some of my questions answered and began the process of starting this business. We got together and decided that the nonprofit would focus on the following areas, education, career, goals, success planning, character development, financial stability, leadership, time management, and relationships. We decided to have values that really mean a lot to us and to other women such as diversity, education, women's rights, equity and inclusion, equality, relationships, and integrity.

How the Book *W*Power is Helping the Nonprofit

When you write a book you can tell your stories on your own terms. A published book gives you a platform to talk about your nonprofit and your cause in the way you see fit, without the filter or influence of the media or anyone else. It's an opportunity to put your organization's best foot forward with you leading the way. No one can tell you what to write in your book. Second, it will create a lot of shareable content for your website and social media channels. A well-made book can create a wealth of content, quotes, stories, potential blog posts, and even imagery that can be shared.

The book gives one credibility as a thought leader. Becoming a published author certainly makes you an expert in your audience's eyes, even if you choose the self-publishing way. Not only can it achieve exposure, but it can also bring in revenue for your nonprofit. If you publish a book that's relevant, interesting, and valuable to your audience, you may find yourself a new revenue stream. I personally give a portion of the revenue from my book sales to my nonprofit monthly. This book can also bring in new supporters and volunteers to your nonprofit. A published book not only raises your personal credibility factor, but it boosts your organization's belief, as well, and introduces your cause to potential new supporters and volunteers. Next, it creates foot-in-the-door opportunities when you send your book to potential companies and organizations you'd like to partner with. Then there's also professional networking that can be very beneficial for you too.

Part Seven: Lessons Learned from Writing This Book

My role

My role in the process of writing this book is to be responsible for everything that goes into the book and especially the great content. I love my role of being the author of this book. My thoughts and words as well as the structure of the book are part of my role. I set the entire process up and I'm responsible for the finished product. My book's purpose is to empower, educate, and inspire my readers, which in turn makes an impact on their knowledge and their lives.

Ingram Sparks Role

Ingram Spark is a print-on-demand publishing company for authors who want to self-publish. Ingram Spark provides you with the tools to successfully publish using their platform. They are one of the best affordable publishers available. They offer free book setup, free resources, and a global distribution network for self-publishing.

Connecting with Facebook Groups

Connecting with other authors, publishers, and illustrators on Facebook is a way to get connected. These are the people who will be helping you when you need help. Most of the time your fans and followers are using Facebook to be in the know of what you're doing and where you are doing it. I highly recommend building your following on Facebook and engaging with your followers and using Facebook to maximize sales, build relationships, and educate people about you and your book.

Survival during the Covid-19 Crisis

There is not too much I can say about writing during this time. Because of the nature of the world crisis, I was able to write, but the focus was more on surviving. I wrote very minimally until I could see that things were improving. Other authors I talked to, wrote all the time, and finished their books during Covid.

The Challenges of Self-Publishing

Everyone will face different challenges depending on where they're at and how much they know before embarking on self-publishing. Self-publishing can be demanding if you have not done it before, but it can be learned in a short timeframe. There are many people that can guide you in the right direction because of their experience and will help make the journey smoother. One of the challenges is the lack of financial support, the other is multitasking, creating an audience, advertising, negative misconceptions from readers, and lack of confidence in work, marketing, and distribution issues. You will wear many hats during this process. Although this process is not physically challenging, it is mentally challenging. Yes, your brain is working day and night nonstop.

The biggest lesson learned from writing this book is you will always start off with your plan, but God will add his plan. The plans I had for writing this book did not go as planned. The reason I say this is because God will interject when he wants to, how he wants to, and why he wants to. I started and stopped many times before getting on the right path. There will be detours along the way. There will be times when you write for hours and other times you write for 30 minutes and put it away for days. You will always have distractions so get used to them and count them all joy because there is a reason for all detours, starts, stops, and hesitations.

The first draft will not be the final draft, especially when you run it through the process of having beta readers or focus groups whichever you call your group. The purpose of both groups is the same. I also learned that ideas would come to you at times when you're not even thinking. I learned that mistakes in the first book will show up when working to correspond the two together.

Some of the research will not provide you with what you need when you need it, and you must be patient. Some of the information you find may not be what you are looking for. The positive lessons learned are if you want a great book that offers value, you may have to think back to the original reason for writing the book.

No matter how much you think you have a great book, you may continue to second-guess yourself and this is not okay. If you find yourself doing that, just stop it and do not continue to second-guess yourself. In the end, you will have a finished product that you can be proud of and everyone else will benefit from it.

<h1 style="text-align:center">Resources</h1>

Malala Fund

National Women's Law Center

Women for Women International

Global Fund for Women

Equality Now

MADRE

Women Deliver

Girls Not Brides

Black Girls Code

She Should Run

Girls on the Run

Magee

Women Called Moses

Black Women's Wall Street

Texas Women's Foundation

I Can Still Shine

Bridges Family Resource

WINGS

Battered Women's Foundation

Create a Table

https://www.postermywall.com/index.php

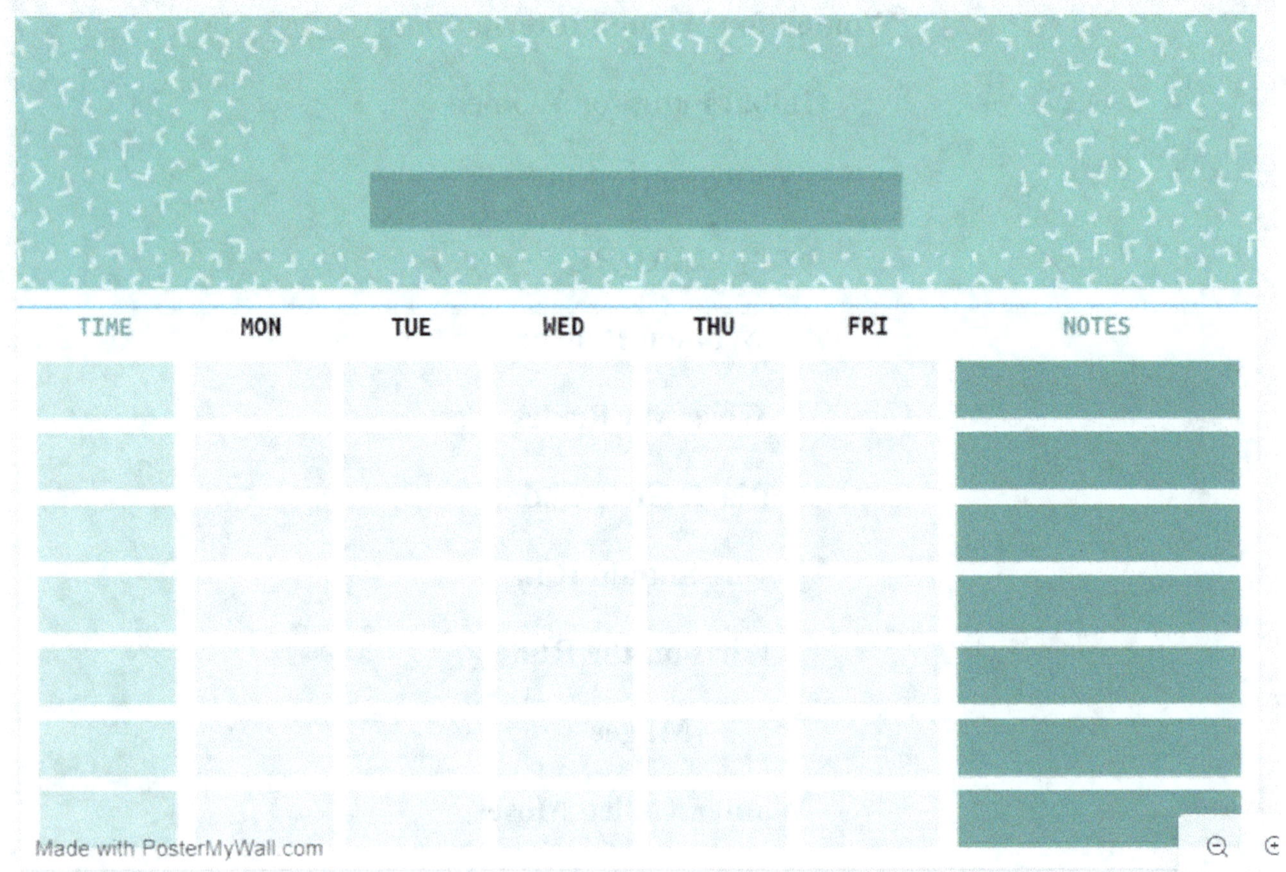

To Do List

1. ____
2. ____
3. ____
4. ____
5. ____
6. ____
7. ____
8. ____
9. ____
10. ____
11. ____
12. ____
13. ____
14. ____
15. ____
16. ____
17. ____
18. ____
19. ____
20. ____
21. ____

ACKNOWLEDGMENTS

I am grateful to my God and Savior Jesus Christ who is the head of my life for allowing me to author this book. I was blessed to write this book with discernment and wisdom from above. I am thankful for my mother, Dorothy Sinegar, who is my biggest fan and continues to support me all the time. I am thankful to all my girlfriends, family, and followers who make it possible for me to write.

I would like to acknowledge my granddaughters, Zoe Priscilla Minor, Savannah Kay Arrington, and Alexandria Rose Minor all of whom I mentor with love.

I am also indebted to my godmother, Beverly Sterns, who pushed me to write the first book. Words are not enough to express how much I truly appreciate you. In addition, I'm grateful for those who helped me with this book, Marilyn Bradford, Amanda Plummer, and my beta-readers.

RECENT SPEAKING ENGAGEMENTS

My Heart On Pages Podcast by LaQuita Parks
Felicha Sinegar Stanley Local Speaker

https://static.wixstatic.com/media/b18eb5_49c9027a107940a9970ef6c06e389c20~mv2.jpg/v1/fill/w_854,h_1104,al_c,q_85,usm_0.66_1.00_0.01,enc_auto/Local%20Author%20Event%20Stanley%20August%202022%20p1%20flyer.jpg

Empowering Writings Annual Creative Connections Conference
https://www.empoweringwritings.com/news-and-events

Sormag's Online Book Festival
https://lashaunda.kartra.com/page/BFPANEL

Trinity River Book Festival sponsored by Docs Bookshop
https://www.thedockbookshop.com/felicha-sinegar-stanley

National Council of Negro Women Dallas Southwest Section
Women Authors Event held at the African American Museum
www.ncnw.org

Contact Information

Contact me for speaking engagements:

Opportunityknocks089@gmail.com

214-878-8169